D1376710

The Science and Technology of SOCCER

The **Science** and
Technology of
Sports

The Science and Technology of SOCCER

James Roland

San Diego, CA

LIBRARY OF CONGRESS CATALOGING-IN-PUBLICATION DATA

Name: Roland, James, author.
Title: The Science and Technology of Soccer/by James Roland.
Description: San Diego, CA: ReferencePoint Press, Inc., 2020. | Series: The Science and Technology of Sports | Audience: Grades: 9 to 12. | Includes bibliographical references and index.
Identifiers: LCCN 2018059970 (print) | LCCN 2019001816 (ebook) |
ISBN 9781682826560 (eBook) | ISBN 9781682826553 (hardback)
Subjects: LCSH: Soccer—Juvenile literature. | Sports sciences—Juvenile literature. | Sports—Technological innovations—Juvenile literature. Classification: LCC GV943.25 (ebook) | LCC GV943.25 .R633 2020 (print) | DDC
796.334—dc23
LC record available at https://lccn.loc.gov/2018059970

CONTENTS

Soccer Gets Its Kicks from Physics

Near the end of a 2016 soccer match between the United States and Costa Rica, US player Christen Press worked her way to a few yards in front of the opposing goal. Facing away from the goal, she took a crossing pass from teammate Tobin Heath, controlled it with the outside of her right foot, spun around, and with her left foot blasted a shot into the left corner of the goal.

The United States Soccer Federation (the governing body of soccer in the United States, also known as U.S. Soccer) named it one of the top ten goals of the year. But it was more than that. In those dazzling few seconds, Press demonstrated the quickness, balance, control, and strength that make soccer known the world over as "the beautiful game."

Indeed, the footwork of soccer players gives the sport a dance-like quality. But soccer is as much the result of mastering the laws of physics as it is a ninety-minute ballet in cleats. Momentum, acceleration, force, and gravity are all at play. Argentina's great Lionel Messi is one of the fastest, most agile soccer players in the world. Messi has become a legend; he slices through defenders at top speed while keeping absolute control of the ball as he charges toward the opponents' goal. Soccer training equipment developer Craig Friedman describes Messi's unique abilities on the field: "He's faster with the ball at his feet than defenders are without the ball."[1]

acceleration
Increase in the rate of speed of an object

Body Motion

So where does Messi's speed come from? And how was Press able to control the soccer ball with each foot while turning around in a split second, surrounded by defenders? One way to start to understand their abilities is through a field of physics called

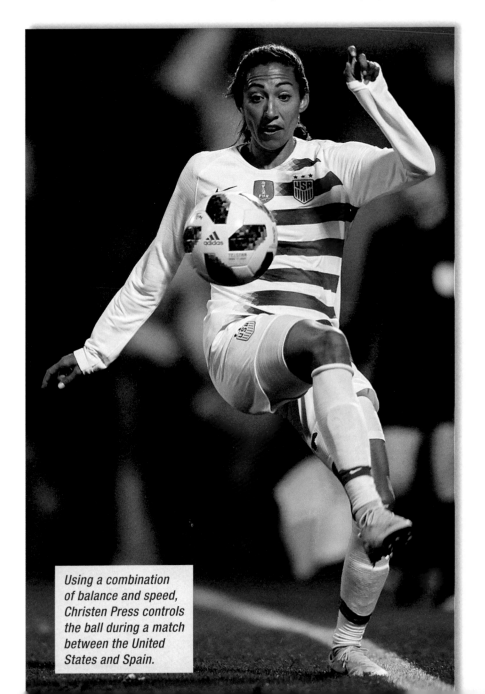

Using a combination of balance and speed, Christen Press controls the ball during a match between the United States and Spain.

biomechanics, the study of motion as it relates to living things. The complex interplay of an athlete's joints, limbs, and muscles is responsible for a symphony of precise yet powerful actions like kicking, heading, running, and jumping.

At 5 feet 6 inches (168 cm), Messi has a lower center of gravity and a shorter running stride than taller players. This allows him to accelerate and decelerate more quickly than a taller player with a longer stride. The shorter stride also makes it easier for Messi to change directions faster in response to the movements of his defenders and teammates. Likewise, Press's famous goal displayed her remarkable athletic agility—the ability to move and change body position quickly while also maintaining balance and control.

Biomechanics is only one of several areas of physics that help illustrate what is happening on the soccer pitch—the name of the playing field in soccer. *Momentum*, for example, is a physics term that describes the amount of motion an object has. The formula for momentum is an object's velocity (or speed in a particular direction) times the object's mass. When a player runs up to kick a soccer ball, momentum is being transferred from the player to the ball. A player can also slow down a ball's momentum when catching it with his or her feet and moving one foot back to slowly put resistance on the ball.

Physics also explains why the ball travels as it does after being kicked. The physics term *projectile motion* describes the movement of an object when the only force acting on it is gravity. The force of gravity prevents a soccer ball from flying straight up into the clouds after being kicked. The angle at which a ball is kicked up, or launched, will be similar to the angle in which it comes down after reaching its maximum height. If a player knows the launch angle, launch speed, and acceleration of gravity (the acceleration for an object moving under the sole influence of gravity), he or she can calculate exactly how high the ball will travel and where it will land.

Excellence from Head to Toe

Of course, in the heat of the action on a soccer pitch, players are not working out complex physics formulas in their head. But through years of playing and practicing, the best players can anticipate how the ball will move and how their opponents and teammates will likely move as well. They can use that anticipation to get their legs, their feet, and the rest of their body responding accordingly. Soccer is a game that requires excellence literally from head to toe. And with advances in equipment, training methods, and sports medicine, soccer is allowing players to perform at levels never seen before. The science and technology of soccer are evolving parts of a game that has thrilled fans around the world for a long time and continues to draw new generations of fans every year.

CHAPTER ONE

Biomechanics of Soccer

Soccer is played in every nation on earth and is the most popular team sport in the world. It is known around the globe as football, but in the United States, to distinguish it from American football, it is called soccer. To excel, players must be able to accelerate, slow down suddenly, change direction in a flash, make a wide variety of kicks, and react to ever-changing circumstances on the pitch. Great players like Portugal's Cristiano Ronaldo, a prolific goal scorer whose dazzling footwork allows him to elude some of the world's best defenders, have all those skills, and they make the game look simple. But there is a lot of science to help explain what is really going on when a player's foot sends the ball soaring over the grass and past a defender.

Muscles in Motion

One of the most famous goals of Ronaldo's legendary career occurred in a 2008 Premier League game between Manchester United and Portsmouth. Early in the first half, Ronaldo took three quick steps and blasted a free kick over a wall of Portsmouth defenders and well out of the reach of goalkeeper David James. A free kick is awarded a team after the opponent commits a certain type of foul. Defenders must stand at least 10 yards (9.1 m) from the spot where a player takes the free kick. Ronaldo and his teammates watched the shot sail over the defenders and into the upper right corner of the goal to cement a victory for his team. "That free-kick against Portsmouth is essentially perfect," writes soccer journalist Tom Victor on the Planet Football website. "There's enough pace on the ball to make sure David James has to anticipate, rather than react, and it flies as close to the top corner as is realistically possible, while dipping right at the last moment. Even if the goalkeeper had dived—something he immediately acknowledged as futile, he would have got nowhere near."[2]

To understand how Ronaldo and other soccer players harness such power and control, it is important to know a little about mechanics. Mechanics is a branch of physics and focuses on the motion or movement of objects. When the object is a living thing,

Portuguese player Cristiano Ronaldo uses both strength and control to deliver powerful, yet precise, kicks.

the study is known as biomechanics, and it explores the movement and interaction of joints, muscles, tendons, ligaments, and even the nervous system. The biomechanics of a soccer kick begin with the approach—the step or steps taken right before the ball is kicked. At the end of his approach against Portsmouth, Ronaldo planted his left foot and brought his right leg back so that the heel almost touched his right hamstring. In biomechanics, this kind of movement is called "swing-limb loading." The hamstring, the group of muscles and tendons in the back of the thigh, is part of the group of muscles that help bend or flex the knee. They are known as knee flexors, and they store energy that can be used for a mighty kick.

As he brought his leg down and forward toward the ball, Ronaldo's knee straightened. He struck the ball cleanly, lifting his kicking leg up to the height of his waist. The knee extensors are the muscles that help straighten the knee, and they include the quadriceps—the powerful set of muscles in the front of the thigh. The straightening of the knee when kicking a soccer ball is an example of eccentric contraction, which is the lengthening of a muscle while it is under tension.

quadriceps
The large group of muscles at the front of the thigh

When kicking the ball, a player can choose to stop his or her foot quickly, essentially punching the ball. This is often done for short, quick passes. But when Ronaldo's foot met the ball, he lifted his foot in such a way to place the ball exactly where he wanted it in the corner of the goal. These two different types of kicks mean the foot may be on the ball five to six milliseconds, or as long as fifteen to sixteen milliseconds with a longer follow-through.

For shots at the goal, a longer follow-through as the body starts to lean forward is helpful. "A shift in weight forwards helps the player to maintain stability, ensuring a more accurate shot," writes Daniel Bousfield, with the Westminster Old Scholars Soccer Club in Australia, in his *Football Kick Biomechanics* blog. "The

Everyone Measures Up on the Pitch

Unlike basketball, in which almost all the best players are much taller than average, soccer has a place for players of just about any height. Players who are taller than average have certain advantages, like a longer running stride or a longer reach. The only position that tends to favor players of a certain height is goalkeeper. Most top goalkeepers are taller than average, simply because there is an advantage in being able to protect more of the goal. Players who are taller or shorter than average—as well as athletes of average height—can be midfielders, forwards, and defensive specialists. Shorter players have the advantage of a lower center of gravity, which lends itself to quickness and greater agility.

At 5 feet 6 inches (168 cm), Argentina's Lionel Messi is considered one of the greatest soccer players of all time. He is known for being able to dart around opponents and find openings in the defense, from which he can score or pass to a teammate for a better shot. "Essentially, footballers with a shorter running stride and lower center of gravity are able to decelerate quickly, anticipate changes in motion and accelerate quickly," writes British fitness expert Ross Edgley.

Ross Edgley, "The Sports Science Behind Lionel Messi's Amazing Dribbling Ability," Bleacher Report, March 6, 2015. www.bleacherreport.com.

follow-through keeps the foot in contact with the ball for longer, which in turn maximizes the transfer of momentum onto the ball and increases its speed."[3]

All the Muscles and Joints

Kicking, running, throwing, and all the other movements required in soccer involve all the body's muscles and joints at some point. For example, the abdominal muscles, the erector spinae (muscles that run along the spine), and the psoas major (muscles that run from the lower back down into the pelvic region) are all involved in stabilizing the torso.

In the upper body, the deltoids (shoulder), biceps (upper arm), and pectorals (chest) help turn the shoulder opposite the kicking foot toward the midline of the body during a kick. And the largest muscle in the body, the gluteus (in the buttocks), helps move the hips in just about every action a soccer player takes on the field—from bending over to help pull up a teammate who has fallen to outrunning a defender, jumping to make a save, and much more.

All of these motions rely on impulses from the brain. Being able to make split-second decisions is essential to soccer success. Researchers believe that some players achieve success in the sport because they can process information faster than the average person. This is often called "reading the game." Superstar players seem to know where to be at all times and what their teammates and opponents are going to do from the start of the game to the final whistle. "There is a certain amount of genius about the great players, and I mean that as an intelligence thing,"[4] says University of Washington neuroscientist Michael Shadlen, who has studied brain activity in athletes.

Becky Sauerbrunn seems to be one of those players. A defender on the U.S. Women's National Team, Sauerbrunn is viewed as one of the smartest players around, given how well she anticipates ball movement and reacts to the action throughout the game. "She is the best defender in the world," says Vlatko Andonovski, who was Sauerbrunn's coach with FC Kansas City of the National Women's Soccer League. "The way she thinks about the game, the way she plays the game, the way she reads the game."[5]

Kicks

As important as game intelligence is to high-level play, it is just one of many fundamentals of soccer. High on the list of other fundamentals is kicking ability. Players use a variety of kicks for different situations. The most commonly used kick when trying to score or making a long pass is known as the instep kick or "laces" kick. The instep is the top of the foot, where a shoe's laces are located. An instep kick can be broken down into six biomechanical phases.

instep
The arched middle portion of the foot in front of the ankle joint

The Instep Kick

The instep kick is central to soccer. The power and accuracy of this kick makes it ideal for goal shots. A successful instep kick involves acceleration, power, and swing in addition to the coordination of moving body parts and proper foot placement and positioning. The biomechanical stages of the instep kick include: approach (1); planting foot (2); backswing (3); hip flexion and knee extension (4); foot contact (5); and follow-through (6).

Source: Bridget Thompson, "What Are the Biomechanical Principles That Optimize and Enhance the Instep Soccer Kick?," *Biomechanics of Soccer Kick* (blog), June 14, 2015. http://biomechancicsofsoccerkick.blogspot.com.

The first phase is the approach angle. When a player approaches the ball before kicking it, he or she comes in at an angle, rather than straight behind the ball. By being at an angle, a player will be able to rotate the hips during the kick. This allows the player to generate more power at the moment of impact, compared to what could be generated by approaching the ball with less movement of the hips.

The second phase of an instep kick is the force produced by what soccer players refer to as the "plant foot." This is the nonkicking foot, the one that is planted firmly on the ground. To

Instep or Toe? Which Is Best?

A soccer player may make dozens of passes in a game, some short, some long. And by the final whistle, he or she could have used every part of both feet in moving the ball along. But is there an advantage in booting the ball with the toe versus the inside part of the foot? It depends on what the player is trying to do. Both types of kicks have their advantages and limitations. For example, kicking the ball with the toe means a player is striking the ball with a smaller surface area—just the tip of the shoe. Compare that to using the entire side of the shoe. With a larger surface area striking the ball, a player can be more accurate with the pass. The side of the foot is better able to control and guide the ball in the right direction. However, because of the leg's biomechanics, the force a player can generate by swinging the leg sideways to pass with the inside part of the foot is much less than with a toe kick, in which a player swings his or her leg back and then down and through the ball. When distance is needed, players generally use the toe or instep. When shorter, more accurate passes are called for, they use the side of the foot.

create maximum force and to help with accuracy, the plant foot is placed 3 to 4 inches (7.6 to 10.2 cm) to the side of the ball, perpendicular to its center. If the plant foot is too far behind or in front of the ball, the player weakens the force put on the shot. It is also harder to maintain balance if the supporting foot is not along the center of the ball.

The next part of an instep kick is the backswing, the moment when the kicking leg swings back prior to its downward movement toward the ball. It may seem like a simple action, but the backswing involves the flexion (bending) of the knee, the extension (straightening) of the hip joint, and the storage of elastic energy in the kicking leg. Elastic energy is another way of describing the potential energy that can be unleashed when an object that has been stretched returns to its normal state. Think of an archer pulling back the string of a bow. That taut string is holding a lot of elastic energy that will send an arrow to its target when the archer lets go. The elastic energy in the kicking leg will soon be used to blast the soccer ball toward its target.

Following the backswing is the downward motion of the leg during a kick. This fourth phase of an instep kick is basically the opposite of the backswing. Now the kicking leg's knee is extending and the hip is flexing. The upper body's movement and position also play a key biomechanical role. The arm on the nonkicking side extends out to the side to provide balance during these few seconds. The elastic energy stored during the backswing is starting to be released as the kicking leg comes down toward the ball.

The fifth phase is the one that gets the most attention. It is the foot-to-ball contact that most directly affects the speed and direction of the ball. Striking the ball lower (closer to the ground) will send it higher in the air, but at a slower speed and with less control over its path. Kicking the ball higher on the instep produces the most speed and control over the direction of the shot. If contact is made more to one side of the foot, the ball will move more slowly and in less of a straight line.

The final phase of the instep kick is the follow-through. By extending the leg, rather than stopping the kick immediately after contact, a player can keep a foot on the ball just a little longer. That can help with better accuracy. It also allows the player to transfer more momentum to the ball to give it more speed. The more soccer players experiment with different body angles and leg speed, the more they learn how to put the ball where they want it without even having to think about the biomechanics involved.

Heads Up

Footwork is central to the sport of soccer, but players use their heads to move the ball, too. Heading the ball is a skill employed by both defensive and offensive players. And few players have done it better than Abby Wambach, a longtime star of the U.S. Women's National Team. When she retired in 2015, she had scored 184 goals in international competition—more than any player in the sport's history. Many of those goals were spectacular headers, including an extra-time goal against Brazil in the 2011 World Cup quarterfinals. In the closing seconds of a tie game, Wambach saw an opening and raced toward Brazil's goal, while teammate Megan Rapinoe dribbled the ball down the other side of the field. From 45 yards (41 m) away, Rapinoe launched a crossing pass that Wambach perfectly timed. With the opposing goalkeeper charging at her, Wambach angled her head to send the ball into the back of the net for the game winner. "To be running that fast to a ball that has to travel that distance—the chances are that you're going to get clocked by the goalkeeper," says Mia Hamm, one of the first stars of U.S.

Liverpool's Joe Gomez leaps to bounce the ball off his forehead. "Heading" a soccer ball requires precise timing as well as flexibility and strength in neck, core, and shoulder muscles.

Women's Soccer. "To be that locked in on the ball and on your technique with the keeper coming out is so courageous. She didn't blink, she didn't take her eye off ball."[6]

A good header does not just happen. It requires keeping an eye on the ball and great timing, but it also demands flexibility and strength in the core, shoulder, and neck muscles. The hip and knee joints are also part of the action. When players head the ball, typically they leap in the air, arch the back, and then snap the neck forward to keep the ball down. The other very important aspect of heading is using the forehead to make direct contact, rather than letting the ball hit the top of the head. A proper header usually ends with a forehead strike of the ball after the whole body is recruited to get in position for that move.

The Hands

Though the feet and head most often touch the ball during a game (as well as the chest and legs at times), the hands are not completely shut out. For players who are not goalkeepers, the only time to use the hands is for a throw-in from out of bounds. And there are very specific rules for throw-ins. The feet have to be on the ground when throwing, and the ball has to be held with both hands and thrown over the head.

Players must have the arm strength to throw the ball far, as well as the accuracy to reach the right teammate. A good throw-in is done at about a 30-degree angle, though it may seem that a 45-degree angle might send the ball farther. Researchers have determined that the shape and musculature of the human body mean that throwing the ball in at an angle a little lower than 45 degrees allows a player to throw it with more speed.

While soccer is primarily a sport of running and kicking, it requires agility and alertness from all parts of the body. For this to occur, joints and muscles must work together as a sort of biomechanical machine. The combination of biomechanics and physical forces such as gravity and acceleration determine the pace and quality of action on the field.

CHAPTER TWO

Physics on the Pitch

The 2002 film *Bend It Like Beckham* tells the story of two teenage soccer players in England. While the title refers to bending the rules of cultural traditions, it is also a reference to British soccer superstar David Beckham and his uncanny skill at curving the ball around a wall of defenders on free kicks. The ability to curve or bend the trajectory of the ball is one of many skills that top soccer players spend years perfecting.

It is also yet another example of how scientific principles help explain parts of the game that many fans may take for granted. Yesim Darici, a physics professor at Florida International University, says that soccer players who understand how the laws of physics affect their game may have a distinct advantage on the pitch. She explains:

trajectory
The path of an object in flight or in motion as a result of forces acting on it

Kicking at the center of the ball with your toes will send it moving in a projectile path. Kicking any other area of the ball with the inside or outside part of your feet will cause it to spin on its axis, and it make the ball's trajectory bend. The soccer players become famous with their bending skills and practice makes perfect, but knowledge is power. We may be looking at a possible research study looking at the importance of learning physics in soccer.[7]

The Magnus Effect

Beckham may not have the university education to explain the physics behind his skills—he did not attend college, having signed his first professional contract at age seventeen—but his genius on the pitch was never in doubt. British researcher Keith Hanna, who joined fellow physicists and football fans from Belgium and Japan in a study of the sport's physics at the height of Beckham's career in 2002, explains:

> The man can carry out a multi-variable physics calculation in his head to compute the exact kick trajectory required, and then execute it perfectly. [Beckham's brain] must be computing some very detailed trajectory calculations in a few seconds purely from instinct and practice. Our computers take a few hours to do the same thing and, although we can now better explain the science of what he does, it is still magical to watch.[8]

Soccer star David Beckham (in white) applies spin as he kicks the ball. Spin causes the ball to curve, or "bend," making it more difficult for opposing players to defend against a kick.

Putting the right spin on the ball is not a skill perfected by only Beckham. Carli Lloyd, of the U.S. Women's team, can kick a curveball as well as anyone. In a 2015 game against Japan, she scored from near midfield, taking a volley, sending it swooping over the defenders' heads, and angling in past an astonished and frustrated Japanese goalkeeper.

The trick to making a soccer ball's path bend in midair is to master the Magnus effect, a term physicists use to explain the concept that for every action there is an equal and opposite reaction—a physics principle known as Isaac Newton's third law of motion. When a player kicks the ball on one side, it starts rotating in that direction around its axis. This action creates a flow of air around the ball. The air that flows in the direction of the spin speeds up, while the air flowing against the spin slows down—the equal and opposite reaction to the action of the forward spin of the ball. The air pressure on the side moving with the spin is lower than the pressure on the opposite side, where air is moving against the spin. This imbalance of air pressure is what causes it to bend to the right or left. Kicking the ball on its right side will cause it to swerve to the left as it slows down. The opposite will occur if a player kicks the ball on its left side.

Another way to understand Newton's third law of motion is to picture a bird in flight. When a bird flaps its wings, it pushes air down, but air is also pushing the bird up, allowing it to fly. In soccer, similar examples of Newton's third law are everywhere. When Manuel Neuer, the acclaimed goalkeeper for Bayern Munich, pushed off the ground to make a diving save on a penalty kick by Real Madrid's striker Kaká in the 2011 Champions League semifinal, Neuer was illustrating this law of physics. When he pushed off the ground with both feet, he was acting on the pitch. But the pitch was also pushing back on him.

More Laws of Motion

Newton's other laws of motion can also be seen on the soccer field. In his first law of motion, Newton stated that an object at rest will remain at rest unless something forces it to move. A 1-pound (454 g) soccer ball, for instance, is likely to sit on the grass without moving until someone kicks it or picks it up. And, according to Newton's first law of motion, an object moving in a straight line will continue in the same direction until something forces it to change. That could be the wind, a foot, or an uneven patch of ground. And when the ball is kicked in the air, it will also continue in a straight line until some other force moves it in a new direction.

air resistance
The force opposing an object and slowing it down as it moves through the air

One force that acts on a soccer ball in flight is called drag or air resistance. Drag actually helps illustrate Newton's second law of motion, which states that the acceleration of an object is dependent on the mass of the object and the force used to move it. A game played in an area where the air is dense and humid requires players to kick the ball harder to get it moving as fast and as far as a game played in an area with less air resistance. This is because the water vapor in the air on a humid day creates more air resistance than dry air.

Similarly, at higher elevations there are fewer molecules of oxygen and other gases in the air to put resistance on a soccer ball in flight. Mexico City's elevation is more than 7,000 feet (2,134 m) above sea level, so there is less drag on a ball than there is in New York City, which is only about 30 feet (9 m) above sea level. This difference can affect the action in a game. At the 2010 World Cup in South Africa, some of the games were played at higher altitudes. Players had to adjust when the ball traveled faster in the thinner atmosphere than it normally does at lower elevations. Even though a person cannot see the difference between the denser air at sea level and the thinner air at higher elevations, a soccer ball will act differently in each setting.

Where Does All That Energy Go?

No matter where a game is played or how much drag is acting on the ball, it carries a certain amount of energy with it. When goalkeeper Erin McLeod wraps her arms around a shot coming at her at 60 miles per hour (97 kph), she is doing much more than saving a goal. She is absorbing energy. The ball carries mechanical energy, a type of kinetic energy associated with objects in motion, like a car zooming down the highway or a flowing river. Along the way, some of that mechanical energy changes into sound energy as the ball whistles through the air and smacks the goalkeeper's gloves. Heat energy is also produced and released into the air and into the goalie's body, such as when McLeod makes another superb save.

kinetic energy
Energy produced by an object's motion

The mechanical energy of a shot is powerful, which is why a goalkeeper often wraps up the ball and rolls with it on the ground—to spread out the absorbed energy. And because energy in the ball is propelling it forward with such force, catching it and rolling to the side on the ground also prevents the keeper from being pushed back into the goal.

McLeod's save is an example of the conservation of energy, a law of physics that states that energy cannot be created or destroyed. It can, though, be transferred from one object to another. One type of energy can be converted into another type of energy. The amount of energy in the universe does not change, but the form the energy takes changes all the time. Sunlight, for instance, can be absorbed by a solar panel on a streetlight during the day and turned into energy to brighten a sidewalk that night.

In soccer, energy is transferring all the time. About 15 percent of the energy stored in a soccer player's leg gets transferred to the ball when kicking it. Much of the remaining energy at contact is used by the hamstring to slow down the leg after contact.

Brazilian goalkeeper Hudson Santos uses the muscles of his arms and torso to absorb the energy that a ball carries from a powerful kick.

Knowing the Angles

Soccer is also a game of angles. Picture a midfielder like Eden Hazard of Chelsea Football Club dribbling the ball toward Liverpool Football Club's goal. He sees teammate Ross Barkley racing down the sideline. To pass the ball to Barkley on the run, Hazard has to calculate where his fellow midfielder will be in a few seconds and kick the ball there, not to where Barkley is at

The Truth of Friction

Imagine a soccer pitch that stretched for miles in every direction. If there were no defenders or goalkeeper getting in the way, what is to keep a ball from rolling along for miles after being kicked? The answer is friction. As the ball rolls along the grass, the grass in turn causes resistance and slows the ball down. Friction works against the motion of the ball and acts in the opposite direction. This is true for any two objects that rub against each other. Aside from affecting the motion of an object, friction also affects the energy of the object that is moving. Moving energy is called kinetic energy. But since energy cannot be created or destroyed, per the law of conservation of energy, friction causes kinetic energy to change its form into heat energy. Picture rubbing two sticks together to create a spark that lights a campfire, or cold hands rubbing together to warm them up. The amount of friction depends on two factors: the roughness of the surface of the objects and the force between the objects. A soccer ball traveling on a smooth dirt patch will generate less friction and roll faster and farther before slowing down than that same ball rolling on grass.

the moment. This means figuring the angle from where Barkley is and where he will be.

Goalkeepers use geometry in a much different way. A standard goal for professional soccer is 8 feet (2.4 m) high and 8 yards (7.3 m) wide. That is a lot of area for a goalkeeper to cover, which is why a keeper learns to study the angles of incoming shots and how his or her location can help reduce the target size for the attackers. To do this, goalkeepers must think in three directions: right, left and above.

No goalkeeper wants to get beaten by having a ball sail over his or her head. The best chance a keeper has to avoid this is to stay close to the goal line and be ready to jump and make a save. If a keeper is too far out in front of the goal, an opposing player can lift the ball over the goalkeeper's head and let the ball fly or bounce into the back of the net. Not even the best World Cup champion keeper can turn around and outrun a fast-moving shot.

The risk of staying too close to the goal line, however, is that the keeper allows the offensive players to move in closer toward that big goal opening, with lots of scoring space to the goalkeeper's right or left. To cut down on a shooter's scoring angles, a goalkeeper can move out toward the ball. Picture a cone with the player controlling the ball at the narrow tip of the cone and the goal at the wide end of the cone. If the goalkeeper stays on the goal line, he or she has a wide area to protect. But by moving toward the ball, the width of the cone (the area the keeper must defend) shrinks.

This is less of a problem for strikers who can really bend the ball around a goalkeeper or other defender. But it is still a wise move for a goalkeeper to give the offense as small a target as possible. Former U.S. Men's National Team goalkeeper Tim Howard constantly moved in front of the net, angling his body as the ball

Goalkeeper Nadine Angerer stretches to deflect a ball before it can enter the net. The ability to leap and stretch improves the player's ability to defend the goal.

moved from right to center to left and back again. His ability to cut down the angles of his opponents helped as he got older and his lateral (side-to-side) movement slowed. "While his lateral agility's suffered with age, his battle-hardened angle-driven goalkeeping is still among the world's best," writes Will Parchman for MLSsoccer.com. "Howard's always been cat-quick, but if you study his keeping it's always his geometry that strikes you first. He cuts down danger like a mathematician. His angles are incredible."[9]

Perception

The players attacking the goal know exactly how big an opening they have, but their brains can fool them sometimes. Soccer players and other athletes admit that when things are going well, the game seems easier. For soccer players on a scoring streak, their target seems to expand. "You see this often. Soccer is like that where a lot of it is played in stages of momentum and rhythm really," says Derek Bell, soccer coach at Lincoln High School in Wisconsin Rapids, Wisconsin. "When things are clicking the field opens up, and it makes everything seem bigger. The goal seems bigger, the field seems bigger."[10]

This is not just a soccer thing. Jessica Witt, a psychology professor at Colorado State University, has researched how athletes in different sports perceive things differently when they are performing at their best. Her studies have found that golfers view the holes as bigger when they are playing well, and softball players say the ball seems bigger when they are on a hitting streak.

It is all part of a psychological principle known as embodied cognition. *Cognition* refers to how the brain learns and processes information, whether it is from a teacher giving a lecture or from seeing a ball or goal when playing sports. The idea behind embodied cognition is that the senses and the body's movements can affect how a person thinks and feels. People who do not exercise and are out of shape may perceive the distance they have to walk to a particular destination as much farther than someone who is in great shape and is physically active.

One Fast Bicycle

Pelé, the Brazilian soccer superstar of the 1960s and 1970s, helped cement his legendary status with a move known as a "bicycle" or "scissors" kick. It is not known whether Pelé actually invented the eye-popping shot—it may go back to the early 1900s or earlier—but he certainly made it famous. To execute a bicycle kick, a player jumps up, leans way back, and kicks his or her legs high in the air just in time to seemingly miraculously strike the ball while it is still several feet off the ground. It is a matter of timing and skill and maybe a little luck. The move starts with the nonkicking leg pushing off from the ground first to help propel the body backward. The arms are extended to the sides for balance, and the eyes are focused on the ball. Because the kicking leg has to travel much farther than it does with a normal soccer kick, it can deliver even more power. This is similar to how much harder and faster an arrow flies if the bowstring is pulled back farther. The player's leg is able to get more momentum with this airborne windup. During the kick, a player's legs are traveling about 1,800 degrees per second. Considering that a full circle is 360 degrees, the speed of a bicycle kick is like making five complete midair circles in one second. To put it in more perspective, that is about the same speed as a helicopter's rotors in flight.

Witt's research suggests that an athlete's visual perception (of a goal, softball, or golf hole) is also affected by his or her performance and abilities. "A future goal is to develop techniques to help athletes see their target differently," Witt says. "Effects of these visual illusions will then lead to improvements in performance."[11]

Helping a soccer player process information in a way that is useful can make a huge difference in the success of an individual and a team. Soccer and other sports at times seem like they are all about action, but the thinking parts of the game cannot be underestimated. The brain is the organ that sends signals for the body to move, but the brain also receives signals when the body is moving. And if a soccer player or other athlete is feeling good and moving well, the brain processes visual signals differently than when an athlete is struggling. For a soccer player who has not scored in a while and is having trouble feeling comfortable on the pitch, the brain perceives the goal and the field as smaller. "When those things aren't really working for you, it can feel pretty cramped,"[12] Witt says.

The mind can indeed play tricks on an athlete, making the game seem easier or tougher. In the same way, many laws of physics can affect the performance of a soccer player. Terms such as *Magnus effect* or *kinetic energy* may not make it into many halftime pep talks by coaches or into news articles about the latest match, but soccer players serve as perfect illustrations every day of a range of scientific phenomena that make the game so phenomenal.

CHAPTER THREE

Equipment Innovations

One of the reasons soccer is played in all parts of the world is that it requires little in the way of special equipment. At its simplest level, all that is needed is a ball and a flat surface on which to play. Goals can be created by placing rocks, cones, or any objects several yards apart. But in today's game, science and technology have found their way into everything from the size of the pitch to the technology that can confirm a controversial goal call to the gear players wear and use every day.

The Pitch

In the densely populated neighborhoods of Bangkok, the crowded capital of Thailand, soccer is the number one sport. But with few large grassy areas in which to build more standard, rectangular pitches, a local real estate developer and other partners have come up with an innovative solution: non-rectangular football fields designed to fit in tight spaces surrounded by homes, businesses, and other buildings. In the Khlong Toei community, kids play soccer on L-shaped, U-shaped, and zigzag pitches, enjoying an unusual twist to the centuries-old game.

Of course, most soccer fields are neat, symmetrical rectangles,100 to 130 yards (91 to 119 m) long and 50 to 100 yards (46 to 91 m) wide. A shorter field tends to favor faster players, while a longer field favors players with more endurance, because more running is required to cover a longer field. A shorter or narrower pitch also leads to more contact between players, because they are fighting for position in a smaller space.

The typical soccer field (pictured) is always a specific length and width. Soccer pitches that have an irregular shape or size might either help or hamper players.

A narrower field can also limit the effectiveness of the wingers—players whose positions are closer to the sidelines. They are usually among the fastest players on a roster and help set up goals by bringing the ball down the side and getting it to the strikers in the middle of the pitch. In 1987 the Rangers Football Club was hosting a game against a team from Kiev, Ukraine. The manager of the Rangers, Graeme Souness, saw two highly skilled and fleet-footed Ukrainian wingers during practice and realized they might be too much for his team. He then instructed his groundskeeper to make the field as narrow as the rules would allow for the next day's game. Souness told the *Guardian* in 2014:

> The pitch didn't have to be a fixed width as long as it was above a certain minimum, so I thought: "Right, I'll make it the absolute minimum." On the Tuesday afternoon the Kiev players trained on the pitch when it was the normal size. On Wednesday night they came out for the match and must have been shocked to discover that, after 15 paces, they were on the touchline . . . it wasn't purist stuff, but it was within the rules.[13]

The Rangers went on to win, 2–1, neutralizing the Ukrainian team's wide-open attack.

A team's style of play can be shaped by field size. In some cases, a smaller or larger field can either help or hurt. Arsenal, one of the most popular teams in the world, used to play at a small but beloved stadium nicknamed Highbury, for the London neighborhood it called home. Former Arsenal manager Arsène Wenger said the smaller pitch worked against his Premier League team, which closely guarded defenders and played very aggressively. "There is something about the size of the pitch at home," he said in 2002.

> It's tight and, of course, we have a dynamic way of playing, everybody defends well and we are a team who put opponents under pressure, so there is more physical contact. On a bigger pitch, you have less contact. It is certainly linked with that. Highbury is very compact.[14]

Grass Versus Artificial Turf

What surface the athletes play on is possibly even more important than pitch size. Most soccer matches around the globe are played on grass. And many athletes prefer this, although grass playing surfaces often have holes and bumps just waiting to sprain a player's ankles. A growing number of soccer pitches worldwide have an artificial turf playing surface. Usually made of nylon or polyethylene fibers, turf has the advantage of providing a perfectly even playing surface with no divots or uneven patches of grass or dirt. And it can survive all types of weather, requiring no watering or chemicals to keep it green.

But it is not universally loved by soccer players. Artificial turf does not provide the same cushioning for the players' feet as grass, nor does it offer as soft a landing for players who trip and fall. The entire 2015 Women's World Cup was played in stadiums with artificial turf, which led to many complaints from athletes. Abby Wambach, for example, said running on turf made it harder to recover and be pain free the next day than when playing on grass. Because turf is more rigid than grass, it absorbs less energy from players as their feet strike the surface. Instead, that energy is returned to the legs of the players, taking a greater toll on their muscles.

Because turf is a harder, smoother surface than grass, players can run faster on it. And, because the more rigid surface absorbs less energy from the ball, balls tend to bounce higher. All of this can make for a more exciting game for fans even as it creates a more challenging environment for athletes.

Shoes

The surface of a soccer pitch not only affects the bounce of the ball and the impact on the muscles. It also determines what the players put on their feet. Soccer shoes—sometimes called boots—that traverse the pitch are fitted with cleats, which are metal or rubber studs on the soles of shoes. It is why these and similar athletic shoes are often referred to simply as cleats.

Cleats serve two very different but equally important purposes. First, cleats give players traction on the grass. In 2007, in front of seventy thousand fans in Rio de Janeiro's famed Maracaña Stadium, Brazil's legendary women's national team star Marta Vieira da Silva (better known simply as Marta) had one of her most acclaimed performances. Just before scoring one of her two goals that day, she sprinted with the ball almost the length of the field, stopped suddenly, shifted her weight from her right foot to her left and back again, and then took off toward her opponents' goal, having left her defender wondering what just happened. What helped the great Marta make those moves were the cleats digging into the pitch just enough to allow her to keep her balance and avoid slipping while making some very slippery moves with the ball.

Indeed, all soccer boots have cleats. Many of those worn by professionals and top youth players have studs that a player can remove and replace with ones of different lengths. These changes are

Old and New at the Same Time

Fans of the 2018 World Cup may have noticed that the soccer balls used in the tournament resembled what is considered a classic "old-school" design. Soccer balls used to be one color and made of leather. Then in the 1970 World Cup in Mexico, a ball with black-and-white pentagons made its internationally televised debut. Instantly, it was a hit and became the image of what soccer balls were supposed to look like. In recent years, more vibrant colors on soccer balls became the norm.

Then in 2018 Adidas decided to bring back its Telstar (named after the first communications satellite) ball that it had debuted in 1970. But the Telstar 18, with its black-and-white color scheme, was about more than nostalgia. It was put through a battery of tests on three continents, checking to see how it performed in temperatures below freezing and above 100°F (37.8°C). The ball was tested at sea level and at high elevations just to see whether it would perform up to the standards of the world's greatest players. It was even fitted with a near-field communication chip that allowed fans to get information about the ball from their smartphones. The next generation of Telstar soccer balls from Adidas is expected to provide fans instantaneous information about trajectory, spin, and much more.

made depending on the height of the grass and other conditions. A wet field may require longer studs for better traction. A special wrench is used to twist off a stud and tighten its replacement.

The other benefit of shoes with cleats is the way they can enhance a player's speed when running. US soccer star Michelle Akers was named by the International Federation of Association Football (FIFA) as one of its top two female players of the twentieth century. One of the reasons for her dominance in soccer was her speed. At 5 feet 10 inches (178 cm), she had a long stride that could outpace most defenders. In the closing minutes of 1991's World Cup final (FIFA's first-ever Women's World Cup), Akers raced past Norway's defenders to take a long pass and score the game winner from a few yards in front of the goal.

Brazilian soccer star Marta Vieira da Silva relies on her cleats to provide just the right amount of traction needed for sudden stops and changes of direction.

Akers's remarkable run was largely possible because of her skill and talent, but she got an assist from her cleats. With only a few little cleats touching the grass with every rapid step, Akers could pick up her feet faster and get down the pitch in time to make history. "Since the cleats stick into the ground instead of the entire foot stepping on it, they allow the players to run faster. The same goes for the cheetah, which sticks its claws into the ground, running almost on its nails," writes Erez Garty of the Davidson Institute of Science Education. "This reduces the cheetah's friction with the ground, allowing it to spring forward."[15]

Gloves

What soccer players put on their feet is among the most important equipment choices they can make. For goalkeepers, though, what they place on their hands may be nearly as significant. A keeper's gloves can make the difference between a big save and a tough loss.

Most goalkeeper gloves extend about 0.5 to 1 inch (1.3 to 2.5 cm) past the end of the fingertips. Oversized gloves make it a little easier to block shots. Soccer goalkeeper gloves also have segmented spines in their fingers that allow the fingers to bend forward when catching or throwing the ball. But the spines do not bend backward, so a keeper's fingers cannot become hyperextended (bending too far in the wrong direction). This is key to preventing one or more fingers from being pushed backward, possibly breaking or dislocating the digits. Stiffer spines mean the gloves can better keep the ball in front of the keeper rather than allow it to power past bent fingers. Goalkeeper gloves also allow the keeper to sling the ball out to teammates. The gloves do not allow for as much pinpoint finger control, but given the size of a soccer ball, small motor skills are not necessary.

hyperextended
When a body part such as an elbow or knee extends beyond the normal range of motion

The gloves themselves are cushioned and made with a combination of natural fibers and synthetic latex foams. Unlike smooth leather gloves from many years ago, modern goalkeeper gloves have palms that are textured or dimpled to make catching and holding on to the ball easier. A thinner palm gives a goalkeeper a better feel for the ball, while more cushioning offers better protection.

synthetic
Made with chemicals to imitate a natural product

Are Helmets in Soccer's Future?

In American football a sturdy helmet and face mask are essential for safety. The helmets even carry the logos of the teams, making them important features of the uniform, not just protective gear. But for a long time, the only headgear in soccer was a goalkeeper's helmet that fits snugly on the head and over the ears with a buckle under the chin. That may be changing. As medical studies continue to pile up evidence of concussion risks in soccer, it is possible that all soccer players will wear helmets of some kind in the near future. In 2004 FIFA made protective headgear an option for all players, but it is not a change many players made.

Amid a growing cry for greater player safety from parents and other soccer advocates, in 2018 the Virginia Tech Helmet Lab submitted twenty-two light-weight but padded helmet designs for safety testing. It was the first testing of helmets for soccer players. On a scale of one to five stars, three helmet models earned a five-star safety rating. That means the helmets were associated with at least a 70 percent reduction in concussion risk. If such promising test results continue, soccer helmets could become standard.

The Ball

The most important piece of equipment in any soccer match is, of course, the ball. A standard soccer ball is 27 to 28 inches (68.6 to 71.1 cm) in circumference and is inflated to a pressure from 8.5 to 15 pounds (3.9 to 6.8 kg) per square inch. It can weigh about 1 pound (454 g). The air pressure inside a soccer ball significantly affects how the ball travels. The greater the pressure inside a ball, the farther it can travel. This is because the surface of the ball is stiffer when the pressure is higher. More energy is transferred to a "stiffer" soccer ball, because little energy is spent deforming the shape of the ball on impact. A soccer ball with less air pressure is softer and will deform more around the foot when kicked. In this instance, energy is spent deforming the shape of the ball rather than pushing the ball harder and faster through the air or across the grass. Thus, an underinflated soccer ball will not travel as far and as fast as a properly inflated ball if both are kicked with the same amount of force.

The surface material of the ball also affects its flight. Synthetic leather covers most current soccer balls. They repel moisture, so there is less drag to slow down their movement. Soccer balls used to be covered in real leather, but because leather absorbs moisture, they often became heavy and lost some of their bounce in wet weather or rolling around on wet grass.

Electronic Eyes on the Ball

Switching from real leather to synthetic leather is but one change from the traditional game to the more modern version of soccer. One of the biggest innovations in recent years is the use of video technology to help cut down on the arguments between coaches and referees, players and referees, and fans of opposing squads.

In soccer the ball must pass completely over the goal line to count as a goal. When the action is fast, the goalkeeper knocks the ball away while it is on the line, or the ball is in the air and gets deflected away from the goal, it can be hard for a referee to make a definitive call. During the 2010 World Cup, England's Frank Lampard appeared to have scored a game-tying goal against Germany with a shot that hit the crossbar and then crossed over the goal line. But referee Jorge Larrionda disallowed the goal, saying it had not crossed completely over the line. England went on to lose the match, but the soccer world may have won an important victory.

By 2014 goal-line technology (GLT) was in place in leagues around the world, including the World Cup. The Lampard non-goal helped usher in the use of technology for controversial scoring chances, but it was one of many disputed goals that had fans and players alike clamoring for a better system. One version of GLT uses antennas to create an electromagnetic field across the front

electromagnetic
Relating to a magnetic field generated by electric currents

of the goal and a ball that is fitted with a microchip. When the ball disturbs the magnetic field, meaning it crosses the goal line, the chip sends a signal to the referee's watch, signaling "goal" or "no goal."

A more commonly used version of GLT uses six high-speed cameras placed around the stadium. The cameras use vision processing to track and record the position of the ball no matter where it goes. Three dots are placed inside the goalposts to help the cameras track the ball more accurately. This precision is crucial to determining whether the referee gets a "goal or "no goal" signal.

Referees will still use their own judgment to call fouls and issue yellow and red cards for player misconduct during a game. Yellow cards are for milder offenses, while a red card gets a player ejected from the game. A player who gets two yellow cards in one game then receives an automatic red card and is sent off the pitch. But game-deciding goal-line calls will be aided by technol-

A technician installs a high-speed camera aimed at the soccer field. Such cameras track the position of the ball, helping referees decide whether a goal has been scored.

ogy. "People will still be emotional about referee decisions, but will be happy that the scandals are over,"[16] says Lukas Brud, secretary of the International Football Association Board.

Yet even with technology in place, the controversies are not over. In a January 2019 Premier League match between Liverpool and Manchester City, Liverpool's Sadio Mané sliced through the middle of the defense and fired a shot on goal. It hit the post and looked as though it would sneak across the goal line. But Manchester City's John Stones cleared the ball away. The referee signaled "no goal," and the GLT confirmed that call. Still, Liverpool fans were outraged after what was their first loss of the season. One fan even started an online petition to review the accuracy of GLT.

Whether it is technology to make the refereeing more accurate or soccer balls that bounce and soar the way players expect, the equipment in and around the game of soccer is always changing. And fans and players will always have strongly held opinions about whether the latest thing is really the best thing for the sport.

CHAPTER FOUR

Common Injuries in Soccer

Given the very physical nature of soccer, with the constant running, kicking, collisions, falling, and heading, it is no surprise that injuries are a major part of the game. Soccer injuries can range from mild muscle strains to more serious problems, such as concussions, broken bones, or major joint damage.

Injuries can affect the outcome of a game or even end a player's career. In 2000 Belgian superstar Luc Nilis was playing in just his third game for Aston Villa of the Premier League when he collided with a goalkeeper as they both raced for a loose ball. Nilis broke his right shin in two places. The injury was so bad that doctors at first thought they might have to amputate his leg. He was able to keep the leg, but he had to retire and trade in his playing days for an early start on his coaching career.

Coaches and trainers take steps to reduce player injuries by putting players through off-season conditioning workouts and resting them when they need it. Fitness training and learning proper running and playing techniques can help reduce the risk of injuries, but in any sport there is always a chance that an athlete can get hurt.

Lower-Body Injuries

The majority of injuries in soccer are those that affect the legs, knees, ankles, or feet. These are known as lower-body or lower-extremity injuries. Two players fighting for the ball are just as likely to kick each other in the leg as they are the ball. Tackles, in which a player extends a leg to knock the ball away from an opponent, can injure either player involved, though the offensive player is usually the victim. Players running at full speed can be tripped or knocked off balance, sending them sprawling to the grass. Player collisions, as Nilis discovered, also lead to injuries.

Of the many types of lower-body injuries that befall soccer players, sprained ankles are among the most common at all levels of soccer. Two opposing players may leap at the same time to head the ball, only to have one player land with his foot on top of his opponent's shoe. Sometimes, what can appear to be a simple twisted ankle can worsen over time. In March 2018 Liverpool's star defender Joe Gomez suffered what appeared to be a sprained ankle in a match against the Netherlands. After some rest and treatment, he returned to the pitch the next month, only to struggle with an increasingly painful injury. In early May he underwent surgery to repair the damaged joint, missing the Champions League final against Real Madrid.

In youth soccer leagues, with fields that are not always level or well maintained, an uneven playing surface can be to blame for a majority of ankle sprains, according to Children's Hospital Los Angeles. On a poorly maintained field, athletes can easily roll an ankle, stretching the outer (or lateral) ligaments of the ankle joint. Ligaments are tough cord-like tissues that hold bones together at a joint. This type of injury is called an inversion injury and can sideline a player for a few days to several weeks, depending on the sprain's severity. Taping an ankle to help stabilize the joint is often done in recovery and as a means of preventing such a sprain.

ligament
A tough, fibrous cord of tissue connecting two bones at a joint

Vulnerable Ligaments

Knee injuries account for about a quarter of all lower-body injuries in soccer. And of those, injuries to the anterior cruciate ligament (ACL) are near the top of the list. The ACL is one of four main ligaments in the knee; these act like ropes to hold the bones in the knee joint together. The ACL is one of the ligaments in the middle of the knee. It is vulnerable to straining and tearing if the knee is hit with great force or if the knee buckles or turns too far too quickly. Injuries to the other ligaments and the meniscus (cartilage in the knee that separates the femur, or thigh bone, from the shin bone) occur too, though at a lower rate than ACL damage.

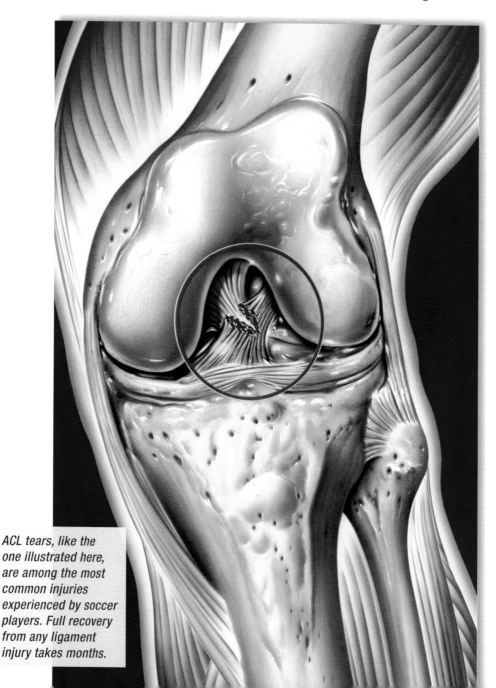

ACL tears, like the one illustrated here, are among the most common injuries experienced by soccer players. Full recovery from any ligament injury takes months.

One of the great challenges in overcoming a ligament injury is the time it takes to fully recover. Soccer players can often come back sooner after a broken bone than from a torn ligament. One reason is that ligaments do not have a lot of blood vessels to deliver oxygen and nutrients helpful for healing. Bones, however, tend to have more blood vessels, which helps them mend faster. Dr. Jennifer Brey, a pediatric orthopedic surgeon in Louisville, Kentucky, says:

> If there is concern for a meniscus or ligament tear, an MRI will need to be ordered by the primary care physician or by an orthopedic surgeon. Initial treatment usually consists of a knee immobilizer, ice and crutches. ACL and meniscus tears typically require surgery and anywhere from three to 12 months of recovery."[17]

Many lower-body soccer injuries can be prevented by making sure players wear properly fitting cleats and learn how to cut and move properly. Staying low to the ground can help, which is why so many players keep their knees bent and lean forward slightly when moving on offense or defense.

Upper-Body Injuries

Wrist and shoulder problems, such as sprains and dislocations, can occur when a player falls with an arm outstretched. Sometimes when players are battling for position, upper-body injuries can occur.

Goalkeepers leaping and landing hard on their upper bodies are often at risk for shoulder injuries. Nick Pope, a goalkeeper for Burnley of the Premier League, dislocated his shoulder challenging an opponent for the ball near his goal in a July 2018 Europa League match. After surgery and months of rehabilitation, he finally returned to the pitch five months later. A dislocated shoulder is obviously quite serious. The more common, yet still painful, shoulder injury is a separation. A separated shoulder occurs when ligaments in the acromioclavicular (AC) joint connecting the collarbone and the shoulder blade stretch too far or tear. A mild, or grade 1, separation can heal with rest and keep a player out for a couple of weeks, while a severe (grade 6) separation will require surgery to repair. The main causes of shoulder separations are falling directly on the shoulder, falling with an outstretched hand, or colliding with another player.

Because collisions are a common cause of serious injuries, young athletes are encouraged to play with kids of approximately the same size. Smaller players are at a heightened risk for injuries playing against taller, heavier opponents.

Heat Injuries

Soccer is usually a warm-weather sport, though many leagues, including the United Kingdom's Premier League, play through the winter. The World Cup, the Olympics, and Major League Soccer, on the other hand, hold many of their matches in the heat of summer. Because soccer is often played in high temperatures, athletes can easily become overheated and dehydrated. The National Collegiate Athletic Association (NCAA) reports that heat injuries are among the top twenty most common soccer injuries, yet they are almost always preventable through proper hydration, rest, and other precautions.

hydration
The absorption of water or other fluids

Heat injuries do not always occur when the temperature hits 90°F (32°C) or higher. A player can become overheated in lower temperatures just by working out hard without a break or proper hydration. Typically, becoming overheated in cold weather is the result of wearing clothes that trap heat and do not allow enough venting. Wearing layers of clothes that can be removed for comfort is the best approach to soccer in the cold.

As for hydration, most youth leagues and school-based soccer teams require water breaks during practice regardless of the weather. Experienced athletes and trainers know the importance

When Do Injuries Occur?

Anytime soccer players take to the pitch, the risk of injury exists. Injuries, especially hamstring injuries, occur more often during a game than in practice. This is the finding of a large study of male college soccer players. Researchers suggest that this is true because players tend to play harder and take more risks when the outcome of the game is on the line. The NCAA report on soccer injuries found that male players were more than three times as likely to get hurt in a game than they were in practice.

Interestingly, the injury rate for preseason exhibition games was higher than for regular season games. That may be partly due to players not being in optimal shape for the preseason. By the time the preseason is over, players are fitter and therefore more protected against injury.

Researchers also found that the majority of injuries occur during interactions between players, either from collisions, slide tackles, or two players struggling for control of the ball. This information helps leaders in the sport focus their efforts in order to reduce injuries in high-risk moments of the season or game.

of drinking water and sports drinks that contain electrolytes—minerals in the body such as sodium and potassium that help keep your body operating efficiently and safely.

Head Injuries

Heading the ball is a key part of offense and defense in soccer. Goals are often scored on headers. And defenders can clear the ball away from the goal with a well-placed header. But striking a moving, 1-pound (454 g) ball with one's head is not a completely harmless way to move the ball. Studies have found that, over time, heading the ball numerous times can lead to brain damage. This is one reason why many youth soccer leagues forbid heading.

"Researchers who've followed soccer players have seen a close relationship between the amount of heading that a player does and brain abnormalities," says Dr. Robert Cantu, a professor of neurosurgery at Boston University School of Medicine. "There've also been studies where researchers compared soccer players to swimmers, and swimmers' brains look perfectly normal while the soccer players' brains had abnormalities in their white matter fiber tracts."[18] The white matter fiber tracts in the brain are the pathways in the brain that connect the various other parts of the brain and allow brain cells to send signals to one another.

Symptoms of brain abnormalities include memory and thinking problems, trouble sleeping, and headaches. Researchers are only now starting to study the long-term effects of heading on the brain health of soccer players. Until more is known or there are changes made, such as lightweight protective headgear, soccer players under age fourteen will be discouraged or prohibited from heading the ball. "Impacts to the head are more damaging under that age, due to a number of structural and metabolic reasons," Cantu says. "The brains of youngsters are not as myelinated as adult brains. Myelin is the coating of the neuron fibers—kind of like coating on a telephone wire. It helps transmission of signals and it also gives neurons much greater strength, so young brains are more vulnerable."[19]

concussion
A brain injury caused by a blow to the head

Concussion awareness has grown to the point that most school and professional teams have what is known as a "concussion protocol." During this process, players are evaluated by medical professionals for signs of damage from a collision or other head injury. Players are urged to be truthful about the symptoms. And if there is any doubt about a player's readiness, he or she is advised to take a break from playing, including skipping the next game.

Symptoms can include severe headaches, as well as changes in mood, thinking skills, and behavior. Coaches and players

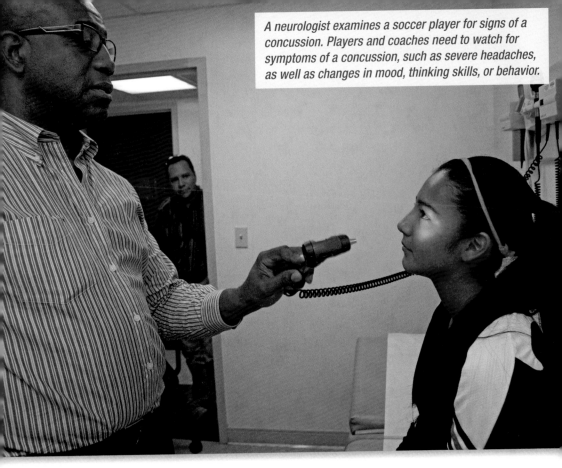

A neurologist examines a soccer player for signs of a concussion. Players and coaches need to watch for symptoms of a concussion, such as severe headaches, as well as changes in mood, thinking skills, or behavior.

should know that a concussion can occur without losing consciousness and that a concussion can result from a traumatic blow to the body, not just the head.

Men, Women, and Injury Risks

Both men and women play soccer at a fast pace, displaying amazing skills. But researchers who look at the nature of soccer injuries have discovered some concerning differences between men and women. Several studies, for example, have found that women soccer players tend to experience ACL tears at a higher rate than men, while male players are more prone to hamstring injuries.

The hamstrings—the group of muscles and tendons in the back of the thighs—are vulnerable to cramps and muscle strains in a game that demands so much running, stopping, and starting. U.S.

ACL Facts and Figures

A sprain or tear of the ACL in the knee is among the most common and serious injuries soccer players face. It can end a season or a career. And according to U.S. Soccer, the risk of a person experiencing an ACL injury goes up significantly if he or she has previously injured an ACL. Interestingly, the risk is higher in the other knee, not the knee that suffered the initial ACL injury. And while ACL injuries are rare among kids before age fourteen, the injury rates climb quickly among high school–age athletes. College soccer players also face their share of ACL injury risks, especially women. About 6 percent of women soccer players in college suffer ACL injuries, compared with about 1 percent of men.

Most ACL injuries occur when the leg is straight, the foot is fixed on the ground, and the player is changing direction. This can put the ACL under considerable strain, raising the risk of a tear. If an ACL tears, the player may hear an audible "pop" sound. That is also the sound of a season ending early.

Soccer reports that about 16 percent of all injuries to male soccer players are hamstring strains, making them among the most common injuries in the sport. A study in the *American Journal of Sports Medicine* found that male soccer players were 64 percent more likely than female players to injure a hamstring.

"In terms of the muscle mechanics, I don't know if there is any gender difference there," says Bing Yu from the physical therapy division at the University of North Carolina–Chapel Hill. "But I know that probably females are more flexible. That means that during the same movement, the male may have a higher (chance of) muscle strain."[20]

More serious than a hamstring strain, though, is a sprained or torn ACL. Many ACL injuries occur without any contact at all. "You have a student athlete plant their foot to quickly change direction, then bam, the ACL tears," says Chicago physical therapist Dr. Marc Gregoy Guillen. "Basically, their knee turns one way and their body goes the other. You'll see this in soccer and football, but also sports like basketball, gymnastics, skiing, and so on."[21] Several major studies in recent years have noted that women soccer players and women in certain other sports, such as gymnastics and track and field, tend to injure their ACLs at much higher rates than men in those sports.

Among the findings of these studies were that when landing after a jump of any kind, women tend to keep their legs straighter than men do. This can put greater strain on the ACL and the entire knee joint. Women's knees also tend to buckle inward, rather than out (which is more common among male athletes), which puts more pressure on the ACL specifically.

Why Biomechanics Is So Important

The better trainers, doctors, coaches, and athletes understand how the body moves and how to protect parts of the body that are especially vulnerable to injury, the safer the game will be. Biomechanics is useful in helping prevent injuries and improve athletic performance.

U.S. Soccer, for example, is using research into a range of joint and muscle injuries as part of its Prevent Injury, Enhance Performance (PEP) Program. Overuse injuries were discovered to be a major issue among kids, whose bodies are still growing. "We started with high school–age athletes," says Holly Silvers, a member of U.S. Soccer Men's and Women's National Medical Team. Along with the Santa Monica Sports Medicine Foundation's Dr. Bert. R. Mandelbaum, Silvers helped develop the PEP Program. She adds, "We realized that was probably a little too late. Bio-mechanically, when we look at these young kids developing, we noticed that there are real deficiencies we can identify even as early as 8 and 9 years old."[22]

Among the recommendations for youth soccer players are giving them more time to recover after games and mixing up the types of drills and activities done throughout the season. Repeating the same exercises and moves can lead to overuse injuries,

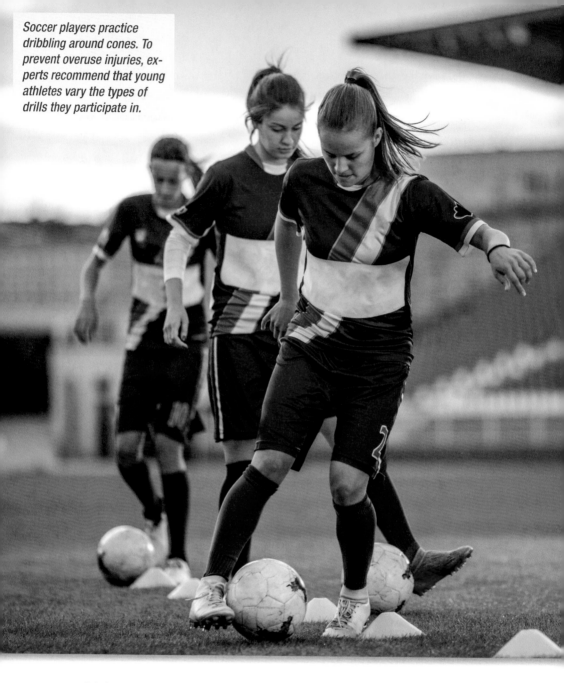

which can become serious over time. Research into the health of young athletes in recent years has caused coaches and trainers to focus more on better hydration, sleep, and nutrition habits throughout the season and during the off-season, too. The PEP Program, for example, urges young athletes to practice smart fitness training in the off-season but not to push themselves so hard that they wind up with muscles strains or injured joints. "There are a lot of things that go into successfully managing these windows of time that we know are too much and hopefully in the end we can start to move away from the current norm to increase the likelihood of success for each individual athlete,"[23] says Danielle Slaton, a former national team member of the Positive Coaching Alliance.

Injury prevention is a high priority for youth leagues and professional leagues alike. Not only is keeping players healthy good for team success and fan enjoyment, it is also necessary for the growth of the game. Parents want their kids to be safe while having fun on the pitch. And of course, the players themselves want to be ready to play at all times.

CHAPTER FIVE

Mind and Body Training

Few team sports require as much running and constant motion as soccer. Soccer players are among the best-conditioned athletes. But the game requires a set of skills that must be practiced again and again. To help prevent skills training from becoming monotonous, soccer players use a variety of drills.

Injury prevention is also a key reason for aggressive and innovative training in the off-season. Kevin Cross of the UVA-HealthSouth Sports Medicine and Rehabilitation Center in Charlottesville, Virginia, notes that hamstring strains occur much more often during preseason practices and during scrimmages, compared to during real games in the middle of the season. He says year-round strength and aerobic conditioning needs to be a greater priority for teams and individual athletes to help cut down on hamstring strains and other common injuries. "The biggest part is appropriate training with regard to cardiovascular and general conditioning training,"[24] Cross says.

Physical Conditioning

When training, soccer players run, run, and then run some more. This is because, other than the goalkeeper, soccer players can run up to 7 miles (11.3 km) over the course of a game. Midfielders, like Chile's dynamic Marcelo Díaz, usually cover the most ground. In the 2014 World Cup, FIFA tracked the distance run by players in all the matches. In just the first four matches, Díaz ran a little more than 32 miles (51.5 km)—about 8 miles

(12.9 km) a game. But that was still a mile or so behind the US national team midfielder Michael Bradley, who covered more than 34 miles (54.7 km) in his first four games of the tournament.

Measuring fitness is done much more scientifically than counting steps and miles. Doctors and sports trainers can use a process called biofeedback to understand how athletes are performing and to help athletes learn to control various functions in the body. Biofeedback uses sensors to monitor brain waves, respiration, heart rate, electrical activity in the muscles, sweat gland function, and body temperature. Using the results of biofeedback, a soccer player could learn, for example, how to lower his or her heart rate by relaxing and reducing anxiety.

biofeedback

A process in which electrical sensors provide information about bodily systems to help a person consciously control those systems

Strength Training

Soccer is not by design a contact sport, but there is plenty of jostling and shoving between opponents throughout the game. So even though soccer players tend to be lean, they are also strong and muscular. For many years, however, weight training and building bigger muscles was not a part of soccer. Coaches feared that muscle-bound players would lose flexibility, speed, and agility.

Today athletes in all sports, including soccer, lift weights or do other resistance training with elastic bands, machines, or other equipment. Muscular strength can actually improve speed, endurance, and all-around performance, while also helping prevent injuries. Naturally, the majority of strength-training exercises in soccer focus on lower-body and core strength. But back and shoulder training is also recommended. Strength training is more intense in the off-season, to allow players to work on skills and plays during the season.

Shawn Arent, an exercise physiologist at Rutgers University, researched the benefits of strength training for soccer players. His studies found that players who built up their muscles performed better and were actually injured less often than prior to participating in a structured weight-training program. He focused his research on the university's women's soccer team, which experienced a 70 percent reduction in injuries after players went through a year of supervised strength training. "When you can keep your players on the pitch," he says, "they can accomplish a lot more."[25]

Soccer players run while wearing waistbands attached to weights. Building muscular strength not only improves speed, endurance, and all-around performance, but also helps prevent injuries.

Research into the causes of muscle strains among soccer players has found that for many athletes, there is a disparity in the strength of their quadriceps and their hamstrings. The study that noted how many more male players than female players suffer hamstring strains showed that many male soccer players had hamstrings that were significantly weaker than their quadriceps. Simply recognizing this difference could help many players avoid missing games due to pulled or severely strained hamstrings. Paul Geisler, an exercise and sports researcher at Ithaca College in New York, says evening out the strength of those two muscle groups may help a lot of players avoid injuries. "It's about coordination and balance," Geisler notes. "An interrelationship between all those muscles allows the elite soccer player to prevent injury and perform well."[26]

The German national team focuses much of its off-season on strength training, which has corresponded to strong showings in the World Cup, including a 2014 championship. In one drill, a player has a heavy resistance attached to a harness he is wearing like a backpack, while the other end is in the hands of teammates who pull on him like a tug-of-war. The player performs side-to-side agility drills, all the while resisting the pull of the other players. It is a simple drill but one that clearly emphasizes the need to balance nimble footwork with muscle and joint strength.

"I expect you're going to start to see that from more countries," Arent says. "They're going to start appreciating the unique power demands of the sport."[27]

stabilization
The process of making something more secure and less likely to fail

Joint Stabilization

Muscular strength is only part of what makes for an exceptional soccer player. Craig Friedman, a former soccer player and sports trainer, says that joint stability is crucial. Joint stability refers to how well someone can control the position or movement of a particular joint. Muscle tone, strong ligaments, and bones with smooth,

Members of Germany's Team HSV use balance pods to strengthen the ligaments in their ankles. Research suggests that strengthening their ankles helps soccer players prevent knee injuries as well.

healthy surfaces within the joint are factors that can improve joint stability. Friedman explains that the quickness and agility of a player such as Lionel Messi comes from qualities like muscle flexibility and strength, as well as joints that allow him to stay balanced while he takes off at full speed. "First you have to be explosive and powerful," Friedman says. "Then, you have to be stable enough through your ankles, hips and torso to be able to deliver that power efficiently into the ground. And finally, you have to deliver the power into the ground in the right direction, and that's where technique comes in."[28] Friedman explains that sprinting drills and lunges can help players with their linear (straight-ahead) speed, while lateral shuffles and lunges can help with multidirectional speed.

Given the fast-paced nature of soccer, players with strong, stable ankle joints may actually avoid injuries to their knees because they are more sure-footed. For the ankles, doctors and trainers recommend exercises such as calf raises and balancing on one foot, first on a stable surface and then on an unstable surface such as a half ball, also known as a balance pod. "There is some evidence that participating in specific balance and strength training can help prevent some ACL injuries,"[29] says pediatric orthopedic surgeon Jennifer Brey.

Skills Training

Newer trends in training are not just about conditioning and fitness but also about dribbling, shooting, passing, and defense. There is even scientific research to support the value of skills training. In one study, Australian researchers found that it was a player's skill, more than speed, strength, and fitness, that has the greatest impact on success in a game. Robbie Wilson, a professor at the University of Queensland School of Biological Sciences and author of the study, explains:

> Higher skill allows players to have a greater impact on the game. Accurate passing and greater ball control are more important for success than high speed, strength and fitness. It may be obvious to soccer fans and coaches that players like Lionel Messi and Neymar [da Silva Santos Jr.] are the best due to their skill. However, 90 per cent of research on soccer players is based on how to improve their speed, strength, and agility—not their skill.[30]

Wilson adds that new training methods are being tested around the world. Some youth programs, for example, have their young players practice on smaller fields with padded sideline walls that allow the balls to bounce right back onto the pitch to keep the action moving all the time. The smaller playing area at the same time demands that the players be precise with their movements and passes. The speeded-up game in a tighter space should make it easier for the players to take their game to the wider spaces of a traditional pitch. Wilson explains:

> Brazilian football academies understand the importance of developing skill in young players, which gives us a great opportunity to test our ideas and find new ways to improve youth training. There are kids with an incredible amount of skill who aren't being selected for teams and training programs because they can't run as fast at nine, 10, or 11 years old. These kids need to be given a chance and the science of skill is on their side.[31]

High-Tech Touches

In soccer any contact a player has with the ball is known as a "touch." The more touches a young player has when learning and practicing the game, the more skilled he or she can become. The Ajax youth soccer academy in the Netherlands is known around the world for a training style that focuses on getting students' feet on the ball as often as possible. "Their main form of training all revolves around players getting literally thousands of touches on the ball daily," writes Carter Lackey of Next Level Soccer, a Texas-based soccer academy. "This allows players to constantly improve all basic physical attributes with the ball at the feet: running with the ball, turning, cutting, passing, shooting, and dribbling."[32]

But getting players at any level that many touches can be a challenge for coaches and for players who want to train on their own. One device used by professional and college teams is a machine that fires smaller-than-regulation soccer balls (known as size-3 balls) at a goalkeeper in rapid succession to improve reflexes. Normally, soccer players use size-5 balls in a game. "I think, after practicing with a size-3 ball, a regulation size-5 ball looks like

Can Video Games Make Soccer Players Think and Move Faster?

Video games often get criticized as time wasters that do not provide any real benefits beyond some mindless entertainment. But when it comes to the EA Sports *FIFA* series, the game on the screen may really help the players on the pitch. Dr. Jan Mayer, the team psychologist for Bundesliga, Germany's top football league, says the *FIFA* video games train young soccer players' brains in many of the same skills they need in the real game. Soccer players need to be able to adjust quickly to changing situations and follow the ball and their opponent simultaneously. These and other skills all get a workout with *FIFA*. "Increasing speed of processing, task switching experience, object tracking," Mayer says. "All this stuff that we need on the field you can improve through actual video game play. And that's a scientific approach we're excited about."

Video game designers have also produced training programs for soccer players and other athletes that are much more focused on actually increasing the brain's processing speed. These developments are still in their early stages, but there are plenty of believers who think a faster brain in front of a screen may just make for a faster player in front of a stadium full of fans.

Quoted in Vice Sports, "Faster in the Head: Can Video Games Make Soccer Players Better?," October 9, 2015. https://sports.vice.com.

a beach ball," says retired professional soccer player Eddie Lewis, who designed the Toca Soccer Training Machine, which fires size-3 balls in rapid succession, like a baseball pitching machine. "When I was at UCLA, I remember watching basketball players working on their three-point shooting on a smaller-than-regulation hoop. Training by doing something that's more difficult, in order to make the real thing easier, makes sense to me."[33]

The Toca machine is one of several devices designed to improve a player's skill. Others include the Football Flick Urban Trainer, which is used by professional teams and schools. It is basically a curved ramp that lets players kick the ball up the ramp so that the curved top sends it back to them at various angles.

Like the Toca machine, this training equipment helps players learn to control a ball coming at them from many different directions. They can work on passing accuracy, developing a touch for short passes, and improving their reaction time.

Instant Feedback

For players who want to know how well they are doing or how fast they are improving, handheld technology is giving them a wealth of information almost instantaneously. The Toca machine, for instance, can be synced with a smartphone or tablet to report how many repetitions a player has performed, which exercises have been completed, and even how many steps have been taken during the workout. "The player can choose from a library of exercises or customize his own routine," Lewis says. "It runs from an app that you download from iTunes."[34]

Of course, there's nothing like athletes seeing themselves in action to learn what is going well and what needs work. Three-dimensional motion-capture technology, like that used to make the *Hobbit* and Marvel movies, provides detailed analysis of a soccer player's movements. Players wear small reflective markers on various joints and parts of their body. Cameras placed strategically around the athlete capture his or her every move from countless angles at 360 frames per second.

A soccer player, coach, or trainer can look at the video and see how an athlete is moving from the front, sides, back—any direction that will help provide information that can be used to improve performance. Motion capture is also used as a teaching tool. EA Sports, maker of the popular *FIFA* and *Madden* sports video games, has put top professionals and kids in motion-capture suits and recorded them doing soccer drills to explain skills through the FIFA games. "By demonstrating exercises using in-game FIFA characters, you're talking to them in a language they understand,"[35] says Sean Dyche, manager of the Premiere League's Burnley football club.

Mental Focus

The mental part of soccer can be just as important as the physical demands of the game. An Australian study found that mental strain affected the accuracy of passes and players' reaction times. To help improve focus, soccer players use pregame techniques such as visualization of plays unfolding in the game. Another widely used method is to have players zero in on their responsibilities, rather than let their focus widen to

Soccer star Lionel Messi focuses his attention on the ball. Messi is known to use meditation before games, which helps him maintain a balance between relaxation and focus.

include the parts of the game they cannot control or are not directly involved in.

Hypnotherapy and meditation are also used by top soccer players to stay mentally sharp. While these types of relaxation and focus exercises might have been scoffed at in the middle of the twentieth century, they are embraced in the twenty-first century as smart ways to conquer the mental challenges of the game.

In 2016 French forward André-Pierre Gignac sought the help of a hypnotherapist after going two months without scoring a goal for his Mexican club, Tigres. In his next game, Gignac scored a

Students Work on Impact-Absorbing Shoes

A group of students studying subjects at Worcester Polytechnic Institute (WPI) came together in 2018 with more in common than an interest in biomechanics and engineering. One of the students was a high school soccer player who saw his younger brother lose five teammates to ACL injuries. Another student suffered a noncontact injury playing lacrosse in high school. And another was a high school skier who watched teammates and opponents also go down with ACL injuries.

But rather than focus on helping athletes after injuries, the WPI students want to design an athletic shoe that will help prevent knee and ankle injuries in the first place. "Prevention is invaluable to these athletes, and wasted money and time can ruin the career of a high schooler and a professional, so repairing the damage is a solution that comes too late," says engineering major Jimmy Muller, the former high school soccer player. "I hope that this project will influence the way the sneaker industry deals with injury prevention technology in their products." In addition to working on designs and experimenting with different materials to help make ankles sturdier in soccer shoes, the students are also seeking investors and interacting with major shoe companies to see their vision of safer soccer footwear come to fruition.

Quoted in Worcester Polytechnic Institute, "Preventing Injuries Is Their Sole Objective," October 16, 2018. www.wpi.edu.

hat trick (three goals in one game). The hypnotherapist, John Milton, says that Gignac did not break his scoring slump because he was hypnotized but because he is a great player who was able—through hypnosis—to experience helpful changes in his metabolism and greater concentration. "The most important thing is a specific breathing," Milton says. "Hypnosis isn't magic. It isn't special powers."[36]

Lionel Messi is known to meditate before games and throughout the season. "In meditation, one looks to develop a balance of effortless relaxation and applied focus," says meditation expert Andy Puddicombe, who cites Messi as a good example of someone who plays with a high level of balance. "But it also helps to develop spatial awareness, mental endurance and pain management."[37]

Puddicombe, who works with several Premier League players, says some of them find pain relief by meditating for just ten minutes after a game. Meditation can also help players learn to relax, which helps reduce inflammation in the body and makes it easier to sleep at night. "Muscles grow and get stronger when we're resting, not when we're exercising," Puddicombe says. "So getting enough of the right kind of rest is essential."[38]

Soccer Science

Scientific and technological innovations are at work in soccer and every sport, improving athletic performance, trying to reduce injuries, and making the game more enjoyable for fans, too. But for all the new tech and all the research into biomechanics, the science of soccer still has its roots in centuries-old scientific principles.

One of these is Newton's second law of motion—how the force of an object depends on its mass and its acceleration. Thomas Kaminski, director of the Athletic Training Education Program at the University of Delaware, is using that law of physics to test his own theory about muscle strength and injury prevention.

He suggests that improving the neck and torso strength of soccer players may help reduce the "whiplash effect" that occurs when a player's head snaps back after heading a fast-moving ball. The sudden, rapid movement of the head after impact is what can damage brain cells. He believes a stronger, sturdier torso and neck can better withstand the force of the ball and reduce the acceleration of the head when it makes contact with the ball.

In 2018 Kaminski launched a study to measure the acceleration of the head when heading a soccer ball. Players ages eleven to thirteen wear sensors that measure cranial acceleration each time they head the ball. They also participate in neck and torso strength training, with the hope that acceleration will decrease over time. "This is going to make the game safer," Kaminski says. "It's simple physics."[39]

SOURCE NOTES

Introduction: Soccer Gets Its Kicks from Physics

1. Quoted in John Dorsey, "Fast as the Flea," ESPN, 2019. www.espn.com.

Chapter One: Biomechanics of Soccer

2. Tom Victor, "Cristiano Ronaldo, His Pompey FK & a Decade of Trying to Top Perfection," Planet Football, January 30, 2018. www.planetfootball.com.
3. Daniel Bousfield, "How Can Football (Soccer) Players Biomechanically Maximise the Free-Kick to Achieve Greater Accuracy and Power?," *Football Kick Biomechanics* (blog), June 18, 2015. https://footballkickbiomechanics.wordpress.com.
4. Quoted in Charlotte Schubert, "Train the Brain for Successful Soccer," *Nature*, June 9, 2006. www.nature.com.
5. Quoted in Kathleen Gier, "With Four FCKC Players, U.S. Women's Soccer Team Is Out to Conquer the World (Cup)," *Kansas City (MO) Star*, June 5, 2015. www.kansascity.com.
6. Quoted in Melanie Jackson, "The Header Heard Round the World," ESPN, June 15, 2015. www.espn.com.

Chapter Two: Physics on the Pitch

7. Quoted in Ayleen Barbel Fattal, "Physics Savvy Is a Soccer Player's Secret Weapon," FIU News, June 28, 2018. www.news.fiu.edu.
8. Quoted in Roger Highfield, "The Mind-Bending Genius of Beckham," *Telegraph* (London), May 20, 2002. www.telegraph.co.uk.
9. Will Parchman, "Eyeing the Future of USA Team Goalkeeping," MLSsoccer.com, August 14, 2017. www.mlssoccer.com.

10. Quoted in Steve Hill, "CWS Soccer Report: Race for Valley Title Remains Tight," Central Wisconsin Sports.net, September 28, 2015. www.centralwisconsinsports.net.

11. Quoted in Rob Waugh, "Could the Force Help You Win at Golf? Just Thinking the Hole Is Bigger Makes You Land 10% More Putts," *Daily Mail* (London), April 4, 2012. www.daily mail.co.uk.

12. Quoted in Hill, "CWS Soccer Report."

Chapter Three: Equipment Innovations

13. Quoted in *Guardian* (Manchester), "Does Size Really Matter? Pochettino Is Not the First to Suffer Pitch Problems," October 29, 2014. www.theguardian.com.

14. Quoted in *Guardian* (Manchester), "Does Size Really Matter?"

15. Erez Garty, "The Physics Behind Soccer Kicks," Davidson Institute of Science Education, February 4, 2015. https://david son.weizmann.ac.il.

16. Quoted in Edgar Alvarez, "FIFA's Tech 'Experiments' Drag Soccer into the Modern Age," Engadget, August 1, 2017. www.engadget.com.

17. Joe Hall, "ACL Injuries, Knee Sprains and Other Soccer Injuries More Common This Time of Year," Norton Children's Hospital, October 17, 2018. nortonchildrens.com.

Chapter Four: Common Injuries in Soccer

18. Quoted in Annie Sneed, "Does Heading a Soccer Ball Cause Brain Damage?," *Scientific American*, June 26, 2014. www .scientificamerican.com.

19. Quoted in Sneed, "Does Heading a Soccer Ball Cause Brain Damage?"

20. Quoted in Genevra Pittman, "Male Players More Prone to Hamstring Strains," Reuters, February 21, 2013. www.reuters .com.

21. Quoted in *Chicago Tribune*, "Take Steps to Lower the Risk of ACL Injury This Sports Season," August 21, 2018. www.chicagotribune.com.
22. Quoted in Mike Woitalla, "Coaches Are in a Powerful Position to Help Kids Stay Healthy," Soccer America, February 23, 2018. socceramerica.com.
23. Quoted in Woitalla, "Coaches Are in a Powerful Position to Help Kids Stay Healthy."

Chapter Five: Mind and Body Training

24. Quoted in Pittman, "Male Players More Prone to Hamstring Strains."
25. Quoted in Daniel Ackerman, "Avoiding the 'Bobblehead Effect': Strength Training Could Help Soccer Players," *Scientific American*, June 29, 2018. www.scientificamerican.com.
26. Quoted in Ackerman, "Avoiding the 'Bobblehead Effect.'"
27. Quoted in Ackerman, "Avoiding the 'Bobblehead Effect.'"
28. Quoted in Dorsey, "Fast as the Flea."
29. Quoted in Hall, "ACL Injuries, Knee Sprains and Other Soccer Injuries More Common This Time of Year."
30. Quoted in University of Queensland, "Soccer Success Is All About Skill," ScienceDaily, November 29, 2017. www.sciencedaily.com.
31. Quoted in University of Queensland, "Soccer Success Is All About Skill."
32. Carter Lackey, "Touches on the Soccer Ball and Why They Are Important," Next Level Soccer, September 12, 2017. www.nextlevelsoccer.
33. Quoted in Jeff Bradley, "High-Tech Touches: Toca Soccer Training Machine," *Sports Illustrated*, April 22, 2014. www.si.com.
34. Quoted in Bradley, "High-Tech Touches."
35. Quoted in Yahoo Sports UK, "EA Sports Gets Behind Premier League Primary Stars Programme," February 8, 2018. https://sports.yahoo.com.

36. Quoted in Associated Press, "French Footballer Andre-Pierre Gignac Ends Two-Month Scoreless Run After Help from Hypnotist," Firstpost, December 15, 2016. www.firstpost.com.

37. Quoted in Ben Welch, "Meditate like Messi," FourFourTwo. www.fourfourtwo.com.

38. Quoted in Welch, "Meditate like Messi."

39. Quoted in Ackerman, "Avoiding the 'Bobblehead Effect.'"

FOR FURTHER RESEARCH

Books

Chest Dugger, *Soccer Analytics: Assess Performance, Tactics, Injuries and Team Formation Through Data Analytics and Statistical Analysis*. Self-published, Amazon Digital Services, 2018.

Andrew Latham, *Soccer Smarts for Kids: 60 Skills, Strategies and Secrets*. Emeryville, CA: Rockridge, 2016.

Emily Jankowski Mahoney, *The Science of Soccer*. New York: PowerKids, 2015.

Charlie Slagle, *Soccer Smart: 75 Skills, Tactics & Mental Exercises to Improve Your Game*. Emeryville, CA: Rockridge, 2018.

Tony Strudwick, *Soccer Science*. Champaign, IL: Human Kinetics, 2016.

Internet Sources

FIFA.com, "The Making of a Football," 2019. https://football -technology.fifa.com.

Erez Garty, "The Physics Behind Soccer Kicks," February 4, 2015. www.davidson.weizmann.ac.il.

Kay, "Football/Soccer a Game of Science," *Scientific Scribbles* (blog), University of Melbourne, October 20, 2017. https://blogs .unimelb.edu.au.

Scientific American, "Science and Soccer's World Cup," June 11, 2014. www.scientificamerican.com.

Ethan Siegel, "The Science of Soccer," *Starts with a Bang!*, Medium, June 18, 2014. https://medium.com.

Websites

FIFA (www.fifa.com). The International Federation of Association Football is the governing body of international soccer (football). This site has information on past and future World Cups, international rankings, rules of the game, soccer news, and articles and videos about a wide range of soccer-related topics.

Football History (www.footballhistory.org). Explore the long and colorful history of soccer (or football, as it is called throughout much of the world) and see how everything from the soccer ball and uniforms to the style of play and the rules themselves have changed over time. There are even quizzes to test your knowledge of soccer trivia and strategy.

Science Buddies (www.sciencebuddies.org/blog/soccer-ball -science). Learn about soccer science and get some great ideas for soccer-related science fair projects. The Geometry of Goal Scoring and Under Pressure: Ball Bouncing Dynamics are just a couple of the projects you can do to explore math and science through the excitement of the world's favorite sport. If you have questions, Science Buddies makes experts available to help online.

Soccer Coach Weekly (www.soccercoachweekly.net). This site has everything you need to know about the game of soccer, including a soccer diet, changing the angle of attack, getting stronger, and learning a wide range of new skills. Coaches pass along new information every month and answer questions from kids looking to learn more about the game and how to improve their own soccer talents.

INDEX

PICTURE CREDITS

Cover: Laszio Szirtesi/Shutterstock.com

7: Jose Breton/NurPhoto/Sipa USA/Newscom

11: AGIF/Shutterstock.com

18: Carlton Myrie/UK Sports P/SIPA

21: Associated Press

25: Andrew Bershaw/Icon Sportswire DJR/Andrew Bershaw/
Icon Sportswire/Newscom

27: Associated Press

32: simonkr

36: Andrew Bershaw/Icon Sportswire DJR/Andrew Bershaw/
Icon Sportswire/Newscom

40: Marijan Murat/picture-alliance/dpa/AP Images

44: John Bavosi/Science Source

49: Walter Michot/TNS/Newscom

52: skynesher

56: Christian Cathisius

58: APN

63: Jack Abuin/ZUMA Press/Newscom

ABOUT THE AUTHOR

James Roland started out as a newspaper reporter more than twenty-five years ago. He then moved on to become an editor, magazine writer, and author.